Musical Equal Temperament and Its Inventor Zhu Zaiyu

Dan Huynh

First Edition: October, 2012.

Published by Dan Huynh.

1 2 3 4 5 6 7

Contents

Foreword

T HIS book is about Zhu Zaiyu's Theory of Equal Temperament in Music, as well as China's scientific and cultural contributions to the art of music. I hope this book will serve as a bridge between Eastern and Western cultures with respect to communication about the origins and evolution of music.

This book will address the musicology and mathematical calculations derived from the Equidistant Tonal System with concise illustrations and will provide easy-to-understand examples for readers to enjoy and appreciate.

I first learned of Equal Temperament in music from Robert Temple's 1986 book, *The Genius of China*. Mr. Temple addressed the Equal Temperament theory using terminology like harmonic resonance, modulation and vibration frequency. As a certified vibration specialist by occupation, these were familiar terms that I encountered on the job, so I felt right at home. More importantly, it made me realize that what we call music was actually founded upon principles of science and mathematics; that the Equal Temperament theory and its accompanying tonal system is what made modern music possible. I was curious and inspired. Over the next two and a half decades, I researched and studied the history and development of Equal Temperament and its inventor, Zhu Zaiyu. I traveled to Qinyang, Henan province, in China and visited the Zhu Zaiyu Memorial Museum. I studied his masterpiece, *The Complete Edition of the Ritual Tone System*. To verify the validity of his Equal Temperament tuning system, I used a Dynamic Signal Analyzer to tune pianos using both the older Mean Tone scale (which was used by the Western world until 1750) and the modern Equal Temperament scale (which is what we use today). I played chords and melodies tuned from the Mean Tone scale, and although it initially sounded fine on the fifth chords, when I played the song, *Tenderly*, the sound was dissonant because certain semitones (E-flat and G-sharp, for example) sounded differently with the singular-keyed Mean Tone tuning than they did in the Equal Temperament scale. From then on, I truly admired the flexibility and freedom that Equal Temperament tuning allowed with respect to changes in key and transposition of melodies.

Equal Temperament tuning was not welcomed by the conservative Ming court officers in the 17th century and was rejected by the autocratic Qing emperors (who thought the new tuning system would distort traditional music and bring disaster to the nation). Indeed, the fate of Equal Temperament in China is best illustrated by the "horse story": The greatest equine appraiser in China was named Be Lo, and he could distinguish the best horse from the rest; only Be Lo could tell which horse was *Qian Li Ma*—the horse that could run the fastest and which had the most stamina. In the case of music, China did not have a Be Lo in those days to recognize and understand the beauty and utility of Equal Temperament. In the West, there were many Be Lo composers and musicians (such as Bach, Beethoven and Mozart) who appreciated Equal Temperament when it was introduced, and who went on to produce countless numbers of wonderful music pieces for the world.

I thank my wife Sabina for her encouragement and support of my work. Special thanks to my son Tom for proof reading and editing of the book.

Thanks are also due to the kind assistance from my son Jim and friend Shane for their software support. I am grateful to Professor Dai Nianzu for his advice and teaching. Last but not least is my recognition to Robert Perry and Arlene Perry for their patient guidance and support in publishing this book, especially Arlene Perry's refined proofreading and thoroughgoing review of the book.

Zhu Zaiyu and the Cultural Heritage

ZAIYU, a Prince of the Ming court, is not a stranger nowadays. His major contribution to the world was using mathematical calculations to create the Equidistant Tonal System, or "Equal Temperament." His visionary invention opened a new stage for the modern Twelve-Tone Equal Temperament musical scale that allowed musicians and composers to freely express their artistic moods and fly in the blue sky with the wings of transposing the melodies and changing the keys.

Zhu Zaiyu equated the 12 tones in an octave to the 12-term Geometric Progression such that each tone represented each term of the Geometric Sequence, correspondingly. From there he determined the common ratio and set up the Equidistant Tonal System. He tried different mathematical schemes to set up this Geometric Progression and even calculated the common ratio to a surprising 25-digit number. He was the first to discover that pipe thickness, pipe diameter, as well as the embouchure direction, could affect the pitches and tones of wind instruments. He crafted a special tuning pitch pipe such that the ascending chromatic tones were proportional to the length of the open-ended pitch pipes based on the common frequency of Equal Temperament. For more than two thousand years, Chinese musicologists and musicians had been unsuccessful in searching for a musical temperament that could perpetually restore the fundamental Yellow Bell (Huang Zhong) pitch after 12 successive spirals of a perfect fifth (ratio 2/3) starting from Yellow Bell; not only did Zhu Zaiyu accomplish this, but he also created the epochal work in Equal Temperament to end the 2000-year search. He titled the numerical values that generated the Musical Equal Temperament as the New Geometric Progression Common Ratio Calculation; the common ratio turned out to be the 12th root of 2 or, in mathematical notation, the $\sqrt[12]{2}$, which is the common frequency ratio for the Equidistant Tonal

System.

Both 2/3 and $\sqrt[12]{2}$ are irrational numbers, so why did the ratio of 2/3 (which was used for musical temperament and tuning for more than 2000 years) fail to restore the fundamental pitch for musical transposition, while the common ratio of $\sqrt[12]{2}$ succeeded? Because the 2/3 ratio is an endless irrational number, $(2/3)^n$ is still an irrational number, and regardless of the integer used for n, $(2/3)^n$ can never equal 2, which represents the fundamental pitch Yellow Bell. On the other hand, although $\sqrt[12]{2}$ is an irrational number, the result for $\sqrt[12]{2}$ after repeated multiplications or divisions will still be multiples of 2. The answer rests on the fact that when n=12, $(\sqrt[12]{2})^n = 2$, because $\sqrt{\sqrt{\sqrt[3]{2}}} = \sqrt[12]{2}$ (or $\sqrt{2} * \sqrt{2} * \sqrt[3]{2} = \sqrt[12]{2}$). Taking advantage of Chinese traditional heritage in music and mathematics, Zhu Zaiyu found the magic number of $\sqrt[12]{2}$, and then relentlessly calculated the 12th root of 2 looking for an accurate result through 25 digits. This demonstrated his remarkable vision, talent and diligence.

Zhu Zaiyu was the first person to write musical scores based on Equal Temperament. He was not only a scientist and musicologist, but also an innovative musical instrument designer. In order to prove the validity of Equal Temperament, he created both the tuning stringed instruments and the tuning wind instrument with accurate pitches. He analyzed and performed textual research on musical instruments made in ancient times. By studying their structure, style, characteristics, tuning method and historical development, he was able to make analytical and edifying conclusions—conclusions that are used today as valuable references for researching the history of musical instruments, such as the bamboo flutes *Xiao* and *Di*, the ancient clay wind instrument *Xun*, the stringed instruments *Qin* and *Se*, and the metal instrument *Bianzhong*.

All of his achievements were recorded in his masterpiece, *The Complete Edition of the Ritual Tone System* or *Yue Lv Quan Shu* 樂律全書. The series was published between 1568-1581 and included 36 books covering not only music and musical temperament, but also instrumental structure, dance, astronomy, calendar, mathematics and physics. The book series has never been translated into any other language, so many people did not know exactly how Zhu Zaiyu figured out the mathematical solution for the Equidistant Tonal System. We are now fortunate to have Dan Huynh's book, *Musical Equal Temperament and Its Inventor Zhu Zaiyu*, which serves the purpose of answering and removing the questions and mystery behind Zhu Zaiyu's theories.

I got acquainted with Mr. Dan Huynh through our common respect and affinity for Zhu Zaiyu; as it turned out, we had mutual goals and interests in science and the arts. Mr. Huynh was a certified vibration specialist who, after retiring, served his motherland by teaching vibration analysis for preventive maintenance in the Three Gorges Hydro Electric Plant. He spent many years researching and writing about Zhu Zaiyu's remarkable accomplishments. Mr. Huynh advised me about a year ago that he discovered that the Circle of Fifths diagram created by Zhu Zaiyu in 1568 was 100 years ahead of the diagram invented by Russian musicologist Nikolai Diletskii, who issued a treatise called *Grammatika musikiyskago peniya* in 1677. I am elate to know he soon will publish the book. I hope the book will promote greater cultural exchange between East and West, and bring more interest and research from musicians, students and scholars.

Dai Nianzu, Senior Fellow
The Chinese Academy of Sciences
December 2011, Beijing

戴念祖
2011年12月8日于北京

Equal Temperament and Piano Tuning

Mr. Dan Huynh has hit the nail on the head with his recently published book on musical equal temperament, *Musical Equal Temperament and Its Inventor Zhu Zaiyu.*

As a music lover and a professional piano tuner, I am appreciative to know the Equal Temperament tuning technique that I have been using for four decades was originally created by a Ming Prince who is rarely known by Western people.

Dan Huynh has carefully constructed the origin of equal temperament. It is brilliantly written with many drawings and original slides from museums to help illustrate Zhu Zaiyu's genius. It is a much needed book to help explain how music has evolved into the 21st century. Dan Huynh's book is a "must read" that people should have in their musical library.

Respectfully,
Alan Pierce RPT
Registered piano technician
Portland, Oregon chapter

Introduction to Equal Temperament

T HE sound of music. Regardless of your culture or background, and whether it be a song on the radio, a concert at Carnegie Hall, or your own singing in the shower, chances are that you appreciate the wondrous and melodious sound of music. But did you ever wonder about who was behind the sound of music as we know it today? Did you ever wonder about the person who created Equal Temperament in music and the pleasing tonal system that composers and musicians have used for four centuries? No, it was not Bach, Beethoven or Mozart; he was not even from Europe. This visionary was a musicologist born in the Central Plains of ancient China in the 16th century and was a star scientist and artist of the Ming Dynasty. His name was Zhu Zaiyu 朱載堉, and he has been recognized by the world as the Music Saint.

Zhu Zaiyu successfully endeavored to create Equal Temperament in music by using mathematical calculations. His creation of the 12-tone Equal Temperament System resolved the mind-boggling problem of musical transposition that puzzled musicians for thousands of years. Starting with a Catholic missionary who sent reports and translated books to the Vatican in the 16th and 17th centuries, Zhu Zaiyu's Equal Temperament System reached Europe over 400 years ago and revolutionized the world of music. Zhu Zaiyu was a learnèd person who tackled very difficult technical problems and his creative spirit and accomplishments were invaluable treasures for all of humankind. This book is about the life of Zhu Zaiyu, as well as China's scientific achievements and cultural history.

The Musicologist planted the seed, but he never thought about the harvest

L ISTENING to music is pleasing; it feels great and helps relieve daily stress. Even light background music enhances the atmosphere. The selected music pieces you hear—be it a Pop song, Jazz, Rock Music, a church hymn or Classical or Chinese Music—all express wonderful melodies with sensational rhythms, colorful accompaniments, modulated variations, harmonious timbres, and smooth chromatic-scale runs. They all take full advantage of the Equal Temperament tuning system that provides total and free expressions of musical modulation and transposition.

Zhu Zaiyu, who created the tuning system that allowed composers and song writers to compose such wonderful music, did not even know how the seeds of Equal Temperament he sowed over 400 years ago would reap such good crops in music. Although he easily could have, he never sat idly by enjoying the luxurious life of a royal prince; all he wanted to do was follow his father's footsteps and actually find the equidistant ritual tonal system for the Emperor and a unified tuning system for folk music. He was the first person to conceptualize the circle of fifths and write music scores based on Equal Temperament, and he also organized a small orchestra to perform the music he composed, using tuned stringed instruments tuned with a tuned pitch pipe.

What Music is

- **Music is science.** It is exact, specific and it demands exact acoustics and harmonic vibrations.
- **Music is mathematics.** Music theorists often use mathematics to understand music. Mathematical laws of harmonics, intervals and rhythms are fundamental not only to our understanding of the world, but to human well-being.
- **Music is a governing tool.** Ancient China's cultural relics, laws and spiritual life were built in part on the foundation of music. Music is for healing sickness and cultivating character. 禮樂治國和谐律调
- **Music is an universal language.** Musical harmonies, rhythms and aesthetic melodies resonate the hearts and minds of human beings.
- **Most of all, Music is art.** Music can generate humanism, feeling and emotion that science cannot duplicate.

A Brief Biography of the Music Sage, Zhu Zaiyu

Z HU ZAIYU (1536-1611) was a ninth generation descendant of Zhu Yuan Zhang, the first emperor of the Ming Dynasty. As a child, Zhu Zaiyu was a genius who understood many subjects by self-study. Later on, the young genius, without any guiding assistance, knew how to make a wind pipe that would play the standard tone of *Huang Zhong* using an exact number of grain kernels to form the pipe length; and he associated different tones with changes in astronomy and the calendar. He liked music and mathematics as a youth. By the age of fifteen, Zhu Zaiyu had attained a solid foundation in science, and he excelled in applying mathematics to convert measuring units of weight, length and volume. He was talented in musicology, and his research skills were at a level that hardly anyone could reach.

A care-free and easy-going person, he lived a humble life. As a prince with royal lineage, he disdained the quest for noble power and refused to raise a sword for frivolous affairs. Zhu Zaiyu's Lordship provided him with personal experiences regarding the cruelty of internal rivalry in the royal court as well as insight into the negative impact of feudalism and the corruption of autocracy. He abdicated his noble rank and dwelled in ordinary accommodations in the country so he could concentrate on his scholastic studies. He was as much admired for his moral character as for his achievements.

Zhu Zaiyu always treated musical tone and musical temperament separately. He explained that *Yue Xue* or Music is a study of sound and

Lv Xue or Temperament is a study of mathematics and measurement (tone generation calculation). He realized the traditional tone generation method, *San Fen Sun Yi*, based on the Arithmetic Progression Law, was illogical for setting up the 12 ritual tones; he originated the mathematical theory for calculating Equal Temperament in 1581, based on The New Geometric Progression Law and it was an equal-tempered tonal system that revolutionized the world of music.

He was a true Renaissance man from the Ming Court who was no doubt a versatile expert on many subjects. In 1581, he published his masterpiece, *The Complete Edition of the Ritual Tone System* or *Yue Lv Quan Shu* 樂律全書, a series that included 36 books and covered Musicology, Mathematics, Acoustics, Measurements, Astronomy and Dancing. As an iconoclast, he unlocked the shackles that forbade tempering of the Court-Controlled Almanac and proposed to revise the erroneous Royal Almanac. In so doing, he eventually opened the door for teamwork between Eastern and Western scientists to develop astronomy research towards the end of the Ming Dynasty. In order to show the practical application of

The Complete Edition
of the Ritual Tone System
written by Zhu Zaiyu
朱載堉著作：樂律全書

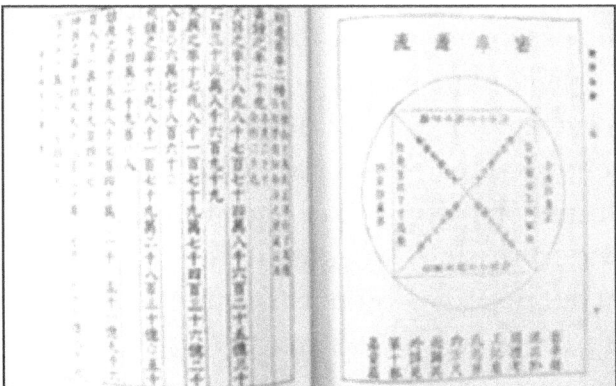

Pages from The Complete Edition of the Ritual Tone System *or* Yue Lv Quan Shu 樂律全書.

his Musical Temperament theory, he wrote music scores based on Equal Temperament; he created the tuning wind instruments and tuning stringed instruments to show the merits of key transposition and melody modulation. He was also the first to construct the circle of fifths diagrams for composers and musicians to modulate to different keys within a composition and to compose and harmonize the melodies.

He roamed around the fields of art and science with his knowledge, wisdom, courage and perseverance; subconsciously sensing his historical mission, he made good use of his cultural heritage and enhanced it further with remarkable accomplishments. He was a "First Achiever" in the world of discovery for China as follows: the first person to invent the Equal Temperament; the first to create accurate instruments, including the stringed zither and the wind-pipe flute; the first to prove and demonstrate the musical temperament theory; the first person to solve the square root with an abacus; the first person to propose and solve the problem of the geometrical series using only a set of numbers; and the first person to write music scores for music using Equal Temperament. He also pioneered the fundamentals of dance and wrote a book summarizing the basics of dance.

Zhu Zaiyu was also known for his contributions to astronomy. His research work not only revitalized the dwindling field of the astronomical calendar, but also opened a new route for future development. His research papers and publications on physics, mathematics, and measurements still exert great influences today. He sought out the truths of nature that rested beyond the boundless sky and he emphasized the use of dialectic, experiment and practice to test truth and theory. He successfully straightened up the historical facts, originated by Song-Yuan rationalism, that had been distorted for centuries, and consequently was able to carve out the everlasting poetry and psalms for us.

Zhu Zaiyu was also a poet. He published the *Admonitory Poems* and created many rhyme verses by adopting the contemporary ballad stanza and folk songs. Zhu Zaiyu was no doubt a versatile expert on many subjects. He was the shining star of art and science that arose between the dusk of ancient China and the dawn of modern China.

As an innovative artist and scientist, he shunned the conservative approach with respect to cultural heritage. He honored the dialectical and experimental methods instead of the investigative practice in dealing with scientific problems; he was a reformer and a creator instead of a conservationist and restorer in working with the arts. He was fearless against authority and was disobedient against rigid disciplines; seeking truth and pursuing knowledge were his great and noble characteristics.

Over time, Prince Zhu Zaiyu became well known in the academic circles of Europe. For a long time his academic achievements were met with cold shoulders and injustice at home. During the last half of the 20th century, many Westerners, presuming that Western Science was superior to that of Eastern Science, slyly insisted that Europeans were the first to discover the Musical Equal Temperament. But careful research into history soon settled this controversial presumption, and several noted Western scholars now agree that 12-tone Equal Temperament was first invented by Zhu Zaiyu and was conveyed to the West where it had great influence on the study of musicology. The famed scholar Dr. Joseph Needham was instrumental in consciously correcting claims that had previously been falsely made. In his book, *Science and Civilization in China*, Dr. Needham stated: "In order to elucidate and illustrate the essence of Equal Temperament, Zhu Zaiyu spent years of effort to refine his books, *The Complete Edition of the Ritual Tone System*; such a profound and major invention cannot be summed up in one treatise or one sentence; Zhu Zaiyu should be honored as the first person who created the Equal Temperament by means of mathematical calculation". Zhu Zaiyu died in the year1611 at the age of 76; he was bestowed posthumously with the title *Duan Qing Shi Zi* (His Excellency The Dauphin of Zheng) by Emperor Shen Zong.

Simple Analogies to emphasize the importance of Equal Temperament on modern music

E VERYTHING you see today had a beginning somewhere, whether it be in sports, art, science or music.

- Before LeBron James, there was Michael Jordan and Dr. J; yet none of them would have become famous stars without the basketball inventor, James Naismith.

- Before Van Gogh, there was Rembrandt, and before him, Michelangelo.

- Before Stephen Hawking, there was Albert Einstein, and before him, Isaac Newton.

- Likewise, we could not have had the Beatles, Elvis or Michael Jackson without Bach, Beethoven and Mozart. But taking it a step further, what most people do not realize is that Bach, Beethoven and Mozart would not have been able to compose such perpetual music without the discovery of Equal Temperament by a Chinese prince named Zhu Zaiyu.

To put it simply, without the genius of Zhu Zaiyu, music as we know it today would not exist.

What is Equal Temperament?

E QUAL Temperament is a musical temperament; it is the standard tuning system for musical instruments. In equal-tempered tunings, an octave is divided into 12 equal semitones in which every pair of adjacent notes or semitones has an identical common frequency ratio. It is the reason why Equal Temperament also is referred to as the Equidistant Temperament.

The word "Temperament" in Musical Temperament means the process of tempering and adjusting through tone calculation the desired tones of a high and low pitch; it denotes the use of a mathematical ratio of intervals to define the octave, the fifth, the fourth, the third and the semitones of a scale where the musical notes or tones have a logical mathematical relationship to each other. Although the "Just" or Pure tones were slightly tempered in this new system, the mathematically correct Equal Temperament revolutionized the world of music in the 18th century because the Equidistant Tonal System provided the total harmonic freedom, melody modulation and key note changes that other tuning systems had failed to achieve in three thousand years. It allowed musicians to play all chords and all intervals within an octave in all keys with pleasing accuracy.

In Equal Temperament the pitch of each successive semitone is determined by either multiplying or dividing the frequency of a note by the common frequency ratio. If multiplied by the common frequency ratio, the result is the frequency of the semitone next higher in pitch. If divided by the common frequency ratio, the result is the frequency of the next lower semitone. An example of these calculations follows on the next page.

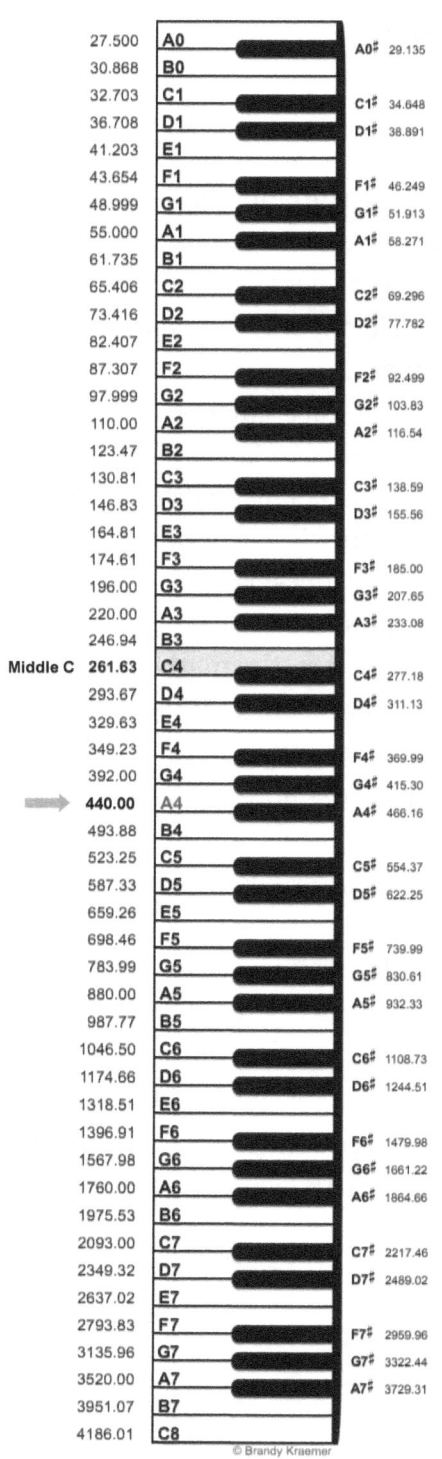

Sample Calculations

$\sqrt[12]{2}$=1.059463094 = the common frequency ratio between each semitone

440 Hz = the standard frequency of the note A(A4) above middle C.

1. Calculating the next higher semitone:
    440x1.059463094=466.16 Hz
    466.16 Hz is the frequency of the next higher semitone from A4, which is A4-sharp (A4♯).
    466.16x1.059463094=493.88 Hz=the frequency of B4, the next higher semitone above A4♯
    493.88x1.059463094=523.25 Hz=the frequency of C5, the note a semitone higher than B4

2. Calculating the next lower semitone:
    440/1.059463094=415.30 Hz=the frequency of the next lower semitone from A4, which is G4-sharp (G4♯)
    415.30/1.059463094=392.00 Hz=the frequency of the next lower semitone, G4
    392.00/1.059463094=369.99 Hz=the frequency of the next lower semitone, F4-sharp (F4♯)

This diagram at the left shows all the 88 notes or semitones on a piano keyboard and their frequencies derived by the method of Equal Temperament tuning. Source: Brandy Kraemer, "Scientific Note Number", 1 October 2012. http://0.tqn.com/d/ piano/1/0/T/F/-/-/Piano-Key-Names-SPN_large.png.

Vibration Signatures

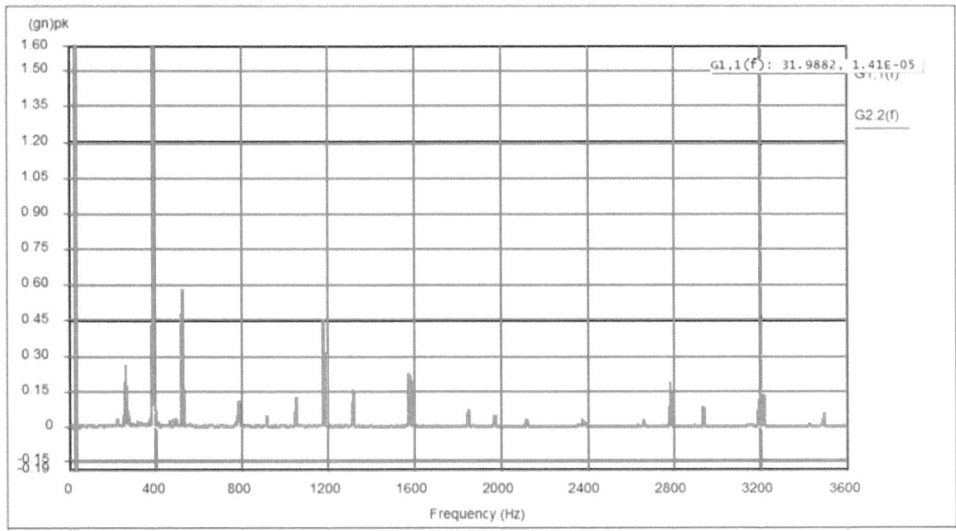

Vibration signature of the fifth interval between the notes C (262 Hz) and G (392 Hz) and its harmonics and rich timbre (overtones) from the piano strings.

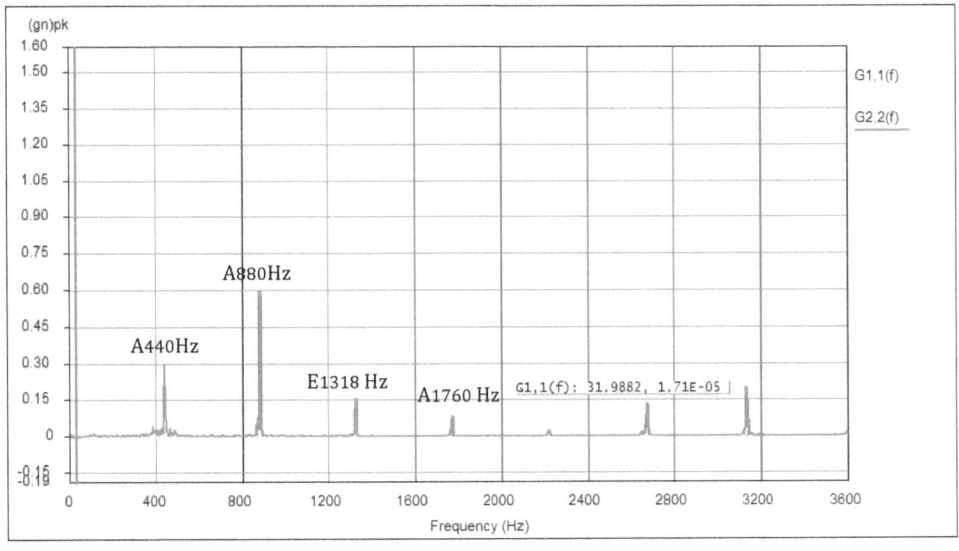

Vibration signatures of the note A (440 Hz) and its harmonics (overtones) from a piano string.

What is so important about Equal Temperament?

S TARTING in the mid-18th century, Equal Temperament became the universal standard tuning system for all the instruments used today. Equal Temperament tuning provides ready transposition of keys and modulation of melody with ease. The music tuned from the Equidistant Tonal System generates pleasing music with sensational overtones and timbres from a series of harmonics and sub-harmonics. It allows musicians to easily modulate to or play in any of the 12 major and 12 minor keys. It also allows the composers of Art music (classical, religious…), Popular music (rock, jazz, romantic, country…) and Folk music (of different countries, regions…) to more freely express their sentiments and artistic moods in their music. It enhances classical music and modern music with harmonious overtones and rich timbres.

Equal Temperament scale tuning replaced the Mean Tone scale, which has inadequate harmony and limited freedom to change keys. Any note of the 12-note equally-divided scale can form a major third interval with the note 4 semitones away or a perfect fifth with the note 7 semitones away. This provides the opportunity for music lovers to make musical improvisation. They can use the music theory and chord progressions to make any kind of music (jazz, pop, rock, folk, gospel and classical) they want. The pleasing music made from Equal Temperament tuning has truly become the universal language and food for the human soul. The chart below shows an example of transposing a scale from the key of C Major to the key of C♯ Major.

Note	C4	C4♯	D4	D4♯	E4	F4	F4♯	G4	G4♯	A4	A4♯	B4	C5
Key of C	Do		Re		Mi	Fa		Sol		La		Ti	Do'
Key of C♯		Do		Re		Mi	Fa		Sol		La		Ti

Western music before and after adopting Equal Temperament

DURING the period before adopting Equal Temperament tuning (500 B.C.–1750 A.D.), Western instruments, such as the harpsichord, were tuned by Pythagorean, Pure tone or Mean tone scales. The music was melodious with simple harmony. It could not transpose the melody into different keys. In order to play in different keys, (say from the C to the G key), musicians had to change to a harpsichord tuned in the G key or tune the instruments to the G key during performances.

The Pythagorean scale is built up from a series of pure fifths, with a ratio of 2:3, drawn together to sound within an octave. The "Just" or Pure tone scale is built up from the intervals in the harmonic series. The Mean tone temperament, also called the natural temperament, is so called because certain intervals like C-E, F-A and G-B were equally divided so that two equal whole tones are between and the beginning and ending notes of the interval are in the ratio of 4:5. Similarly, the intervals of E-G and B-D had an identical frequency ratio of 6:5. The Mean tone scale was the first tempered scale, but it could not meet the goal of transposing the melody or modulating freely. It could allow the pianist or organist to play only 6 keys in one single tuning. The Pythagorean, Pure tone and unequal-tempered Mean tone tuning systems maintain the exact interval-ratio rule for the main intervals, while Equal Temperament departs from that outmoded standard.

Equal Temperament is the ultimate compromise; the 12-tone scale does not produce a perfect or pure Fifth, but for the purpose of musical modulation and key transposition, it slightly "tempers" all the just intervals. The 19th century German physicist and musicologist, Hermann von Helmholtz, said in his book, *On the Sensations of Tone as a Physiological Basis for the Theory of Music*, "Tempered intonation was first developed on the pianoforte and hence gradually transferred to other instruments; now on the pianoforte circumstances really favor the "concealment" of the imperfection due to temperament. The tones of the piano are very loud only at the moment of striking and their loudness rapidly diminished." Zhu Zaiyu did not realize his Equal Temperament scale "tempered" the Western traditional Mean tone scale. He just wanted to build the Equidistant Tonal System with a common frequency ratio based on the mathematical calculation to restore the fundamental Yellow Bell (*Huang Zhong*) pitch after 12 successive spirals of a perfect fifth starting from Yellow Bell.

Conveyed to Europe by Italian missionaries (Matteo Ricci… etc.) around 1581-1620, Equal Temperament created a musical revolution in Europe. Documents show that Father Ricci read the book, *Lv Li Rong Tong* 律禮融通 (New Discourse on Calendrical Science and Ritual Tone System), written by Zhu Zaiyu and that he sent the letters and translated books back to the Vatican in Rome. European scholars and musicians could certainly have gotten the ritual tonal calculations and musicology from his reports.

J. S. Bach liked the harmonious sound and dynamic response of the pianoforte, invented by Italian Bartolomeo Cristofori around 1700 and improved by German Gottfried Silbermann in 1726. It was believed the pianoforte was tuned with Well or Equal Temperament so that it was possible to play music in most major or minor keys. Bach liked the new tuning and he wrote the first twenty-four preludes and fugues in each of the major and minor keys to demonstrate the musical possibilities of Well Temperament; twenty years later, he wrote another twenty-four pieces which along with the first 24 are now referred to as the "Famous 48". The 48 Well-Tempered Clavier pieces do not include the "modulation" made available by Equal Temperament, but instead demonstrate the ability of a single instrument in "well-tempered tuning" to play in all 24 keys without having to be retuned to every new key. Bach has been credited for promoting Equal Temperament with his "Famous 48".

After 1750, Equal Temperament tuning became standard during the late Classical and early Romantic eras. Beethoven, Mozart, Schubert, Chopin and other great composers composed their everlasting music for the world based on this tuning standard. It is in the environment of Equal Temperament that the new styles of symmetrical tonality and polytonality and Jazz developed and flourished.

Mersenne and Stevin's Equal Temperament Proposal

WESTERN writers of music proposed different methods in resolving the distorted intonation inherent in tuning systems based on fixed or rational ratios of 2:3, 3:4, 4:5 to form the fifth, the fourth and the third intervals, respectively. By the mid-17th century, they still hunted for a tuning system that allowed modulating the music keys. Marin Mersenne (1588-1648) addressed the Equal Temperament in his magnum opus, *Harmonie Universelle*, in 1637; he gave the number 1.05946 as the frequency ratio of the adjacent notes saying this was the method for an acceptably equalized temperament. However, he did not provide any reference to the source or the author of this numerical figure. Neither did he mention musical transposition and modulation.

Simon Stevin (1548-1620), a Flemish mathematician and military engineer, published a treatise about Equirational Intervals and calculations for a 12 equidistant tone system. He also presented a method of calculating the common ratio of Equal Temperament using the 12th root of the fractional number ½: $\sqrt[12]{1/2}$ =1/1.0595. Due to the insufficient accuracy of his calculation, many of the numbers he obtained were off by one or two units from the correct values. His computed result provided only 4 decimal points in the common ratio, which was far from the accurate result of 1.059463094…. Simon Stevin's treatise was written about 1596-1600, but the manuscript was not discovered until 1838. Neither Mersenne nor Stevin proved the proposed theory with detailed calculations or tuning instruments.

J. Murray Bardour, the author of *Tuning and Temperament: A Historical Survey*, written in 1951 and reissued in 2004, summed up the inventor of Equal Temperament with this statement: "The first known appearance in print of the correct figures for equal temperament was in China, where Prince Zhu Zaiyu's brilliant solution remains an enigma". Hermann von Helmholtz, in 1863, also wrote in *On the Sensations of Tone as a Physiological Basis for the Theory of Music* that a Chinese prince introduced a scale of seven notes, and that the division of the octave into twelve semitones was discovered in China.

China's cultural objects, laws and spiritual civilization essentially build on the foundation of music

1. **Cultural Objects and Laws 法度文物**

   The first Emperor, Yellow Emperor, set up the standard tone *Gong* 宮 from a bamboo pitch pipe, lined the pipe with 90 millets 黍 for the standard length , filled the pipe with 1200 millets for the standard volume.... It showed that the standard tone generator was also used to set standard length, weight and volume measures in ancient China.

2. **Spiritual Civilization 精神思想**

   Starting in the 5th century B.C., Confucius' teaching doctrines emphasized the importance of music education stating that "To educate somebody, you should start from poems, emphasize ceremonies, and finish with music." Ritual music with proper tones was seen as central to the harmony and longevity of the state in ancient China. Confucius thought that harmony, rhythms and sense of beauty were the essential factors for edifying and educating people.

3. **Ritual Music 儀式音樂**

   The Zhou Dynasty (1000–256 B.C.) was the first dynasty to lay down rules of "rites" (sacrificial ceremonies, court protocol, etc.) and "music" (music and dancing which accompanied ceremony). Music best reflected a nation's manners, and in good times, authority was manifested quite as much in rites and ceremonies as in laws and pronouncements. It was believed when the music is wild and discordant, it showed the nation is in confusion. The system of rites and music endured for more than 2,000. years.

Chinese Music

THE Chinese were the first to understand musical timbre. Lu Ju of the Western Zhou Dynasty (1046-771 B.C.) mentioned that striking the string of a zither would resonate the similar string of another zither located in the next room. By studying the production of timbre on the strings of a zither (*qin* 琴) in the third century A.D, the Chinese have long appreciated the perfect harmonious sound and overtones of the perfect fifth that resonated from vibrating strings above a sound board which was specially chosen.

The Fifth was the basis of Chinese Music. Two strings with relative lengths in a 3:2 ratio produced the two tones forming the harmonious perfect fifth; this is the most pleasing consonance of two notes sounded together. Other pleasing tones are the Unison (two notes in a ratio of 1:1) and the Octave (a ratio of 1:2).

The Gu Qin.

Chinese fundamental music was based on a 5-tone scale, the notes of which are *Gong* (宮), *Shang* (商), *Jue* (角), *Zheng* (徵), *Yu* (羽), which correspond to the notes in the modern tonal scale identified by the Solfege method as Do, Re, Mi, Sol, La. The resulting scale is known as the pentatonic scale. 5-tone scale music was widely practiced because it consisted of harmonious whole tones; use of the half-tones, like Fa and Ti, were not included. The melody created by the 5-tone scale signified harmony and rhythm of the civilized society in ancient China. Harmony in music also denoted harmonious relationships among the king and ministers, politicians, family members and with neighboring countries. Rhythm in music also denoted rhythmic order in daily life, social activities and seasonal harvest.

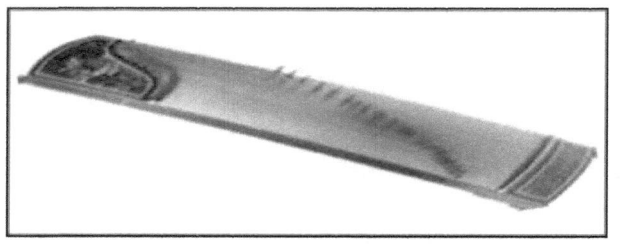

The Gu Zheng.

Traditional music mostly used 5-tone scales based on each of the 12 ritual tones or *Lv* Pitches as the key note. (This is different from the Western semitone concept.) 7-tone music, formed by adding *Bian Zheng* (变徵) or Fi (Fa♯) and *Bian Gong* (变宫) or Ti, also was practiced, but only when there was symphony string music involved. The 7-tone scale is *Gong* (Do), *Shang* (Re), *Jue* (Mi), *Bian Zheng* (Fi or Fa♯), *Zheng* (Sol), *Yu* (La), *Bian Gong* (Ti).

Traditional music in China is played on solo instruments or in small ensembles of plucked and bowed stringed instruments (like *Gu Zheng* and *Erhu*), flutes, cymbals, gongs and drums. Chinese orchestras traditionally consist of bowed strings (*Erhu*), woodwinds (*Xiao* and *Di*), plucked strings (*Pipa*, *Gu Qin*, *Gu Zheng* and *Se*) and percussion (*Zhong* and *Gu*). Bamboo pipes and *Gu Qin* are among the oldest known musical instruments from China.

12-tone Ritual Music

T HE study of music in ancient China is called *Yue Lv* 樂律学；
music is a subject of art known as *Yue Xue* 樂学. It is about
standard tone, melody, tone sensation and music scores. Music is
also a subject of science known as *Lv Xue* 律学. In this context it is
about the tone accuracy, tone generation and temperament of music
based on mathematical calculation.

The development process of musical temperament reflected
the history of Chinese music in ancient China. Chinese music, since
the Western Zhou Dynasty (1046–771 B.C.), had been based on the
concept of music harmonizing heaven and earth and the
concordance of musical temperament and the calendrical system just
like the 12 ritual tones were concordant with the 12 months of the
year. It was essential to have ritual music accompanying the court
ceremonies and protocol when the rite of worshiping heaven and
earth was performed. The harmony and rhythms of the ritual music
(*Yue Lv* 樂律) based on the perfect fifth (two tones forming the 3:2
ratio) signified the harmony and seasonal rhythms of heaven and
earth. It then followed that the process of tone generation using the
principle of the 3:2 ratio must also naturally incorporate the
standard of concordant harmony between heaven and earth.

San Fen Sun Yi 三分损益, the process or a formula of
alternatingly subtracting and adding one-third of the string or pitch
pipe length for generating the 12 ritual tones, had been widely
practiced in the history of Chinese music for 2000 years. The 12
ritual tones or 12 *Lv* pitches in an octave are divided into 6 *Yin Lv*
pitches (*Da Lv, Jia Zhong, Zhong Lv, Lin Zhong, Nan Lv, Ying Zhong*)
and 6 *Yang Lv* pitches (*Huang Zhong, Tai Zhu, Gu Xie, Rui Bin, Yi Ze,
Wu Yi*). Each of the 12 *Lv* pitches was designated to serve as the
fundamental pitch for the performance of the ritual music in a

certain month. In other words, each pitch can be used as the fundamental pitch in a 5-tone or 7-tone scale.

Please refer to the table comparing the relationship of the 12 Ritual Tones and their length ratios using the *San Fen Sun Yi* process versus the Piano chromatic scale based on Equal Temperament appearing on page 26. *Huang Zhong* is shown as the fundamental pitch or *Gong* tone like Do is called the fundamental pitch in the key of C in the Solfège method. Similarly, *Tai Zhu* is the *Shang* tone like Re, *Gu Xie* is the *Jue* tone like Mi, *Lin Zhong* is the *Zheng* tone like Sol and *Nan Lv* is the *Yu* tone like La. If *Tai Zhu* is used as the fundamental pitch or *Gong* tone, called Do in the Solfège method in the key of D, then *Gu Xie* is the *Shang* tone or Re, *Rui Bin* is the *Jue* tone or Mi, *Nan Lv* is the *Zheng* tone or Sol and *Ying Zhong* is the *Yu* tone or La.

In addition, the tone generation process must be cyclic like the 12 cycling months of each lunar year, and the last tone of this process must be a replication of the first except it is just one octave higher. The transposition of the fundamental tone through the 12 semitone series is what the ancient Chinese called *Xuan Xiang Wei Gong* 旋相为宫, which means cycling or alternating the fundamental note. The table on page 25 shows the notes for each 7-tone scale produced by cycling the fundamental tone (*Gong* or Do) of the 7-tone scale through all the 12 ritual tones.

Subtracting and adding one third — the *San Fen Sun Yi* tuning process

ANCIENT Chinese believed thus: the 2:3 ratio was consistently applicable in the process of generating tones for the ritual music. The process of *San Fen Sun Yi* 三分损益,or a formula of alternatingly subtracting and adding one-third of the string length for generating the 12 ritual tones, had been widely practiced in the history of Chinese music for 2000 years. The pleasing chords of the Fifth, the Fourth and the Third intervals could be obtained through the rational ratios of 2:3, 3:4 and 4:5, respectively, as they provide the acceptable notes for the 5-tone and 7-tone music scales. However, the 12-tone scale created by *San Fen Sun Yi* was not an equal-distant tonal system; it failed to return to the fundamental Yellow Bell (*Huang Zhong*) pitch, through mathematical calculation, after 12 successive iterations of a perfect Fifth starting from the Yellow Bell. The court musicians of a new dynasty always blamed the fall of the previous dynasty for the discordance of the ritual music.

Both the Western Mean tone and China's *San Fen Sun Yi* tuning processes provided practical usages without logical theory. However, neither utilized Equal Temperament which enhanced the music with transposed melodies and harmonies. Neither process could freely transpose melodies to any key or play the major scale in any key. It was impossible for a C-key instrument to play in another scale without using Equal Temperament tuning. The following diagrams and tables detail the tone calculations using the *San Fen Sun Yi* tone generation process, showing the calculation error and how the results differ from Equal Temperament tuning.

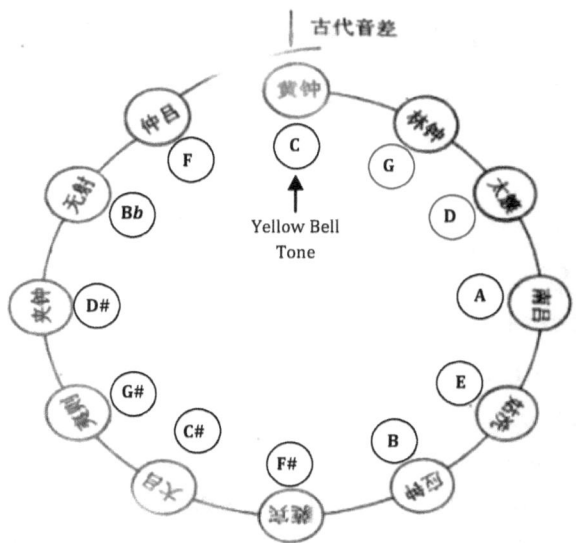

图 7 - 1 　 三分损益五度圈与古代音差

The diagram above shows the calculation error using the San Fen Sun Yi *tone generation process. Starting from the fundamental tone, Yellow Bell, the spiral of Fifths fails to return to the same starting tone—the same pitch only in a different octave; it fails to complete the circle.*

十二律管圖（圖一續）

中國

二七

7音階 7-Tone Scale	地支 Earth Branches	San Fen Sun Yi 三分損益	Equal Temperament 十二均律		宮 Gong Do	商 Shang Re	角 Jue Mi	變徵 Bian Zheng Fi (or Fa#)	徵 Zheng Sol	羽 Yu La	變宮 Bian Gong Ti
	子	1	1	C	黃鐘	太簇	姑洗	蕤賓	林鐘	南呂	應鐘
	丑	.9364	.9438	C#	大呂	夾鐘	中呂	林鐘	夷則	無射	黃鐘
十二律	寅	.8888	.8908	D	太簇	姑洗	蕤賓	夷則	南呂	應鐘	大呂
	卯	.8323	.8408	Eb	夾鐘	中呂	林鐘	南呂	無射	黃鐘	太簇
	辰	.7901	.7937	E	姑洗	蕤賓	夷則	無射	應鐘	大呂	夾鐘
	巳	.7399	.7491	F	中呂	林鐘	南呂	應鐘	黃鐘	太簇	姑洗
12 Ritual Tones	午	.7023	.7071	F#	蕤賓	夷則	無射	黃鐘	大呂	夾鐘	中呂
	未	.6666	.6674	G	林鐘	南呂	應鐘	大呂	太簇	姑洗	蕤賓
	申	.6242	.6299	G#	夷則	無射	黃鐘	太簇	夾鐘	中呂	林鐘
	酉	.5925	.5946	A	南呂	應鐘	大呂	夾鐘	姑洗	蕤賓	夷則
	戌	.5549	.5612	Bb	無射	黃鐘	太簇	姑洗	中呂	林鐘	南呂
	亥	.5267	.5297	B	應鐘	大呂	夾鐘	中呂	蕤賓	夷則	無射
		.4932	.5000	C'	黃鐘 Qing Huang Zhong						

Generation of the 12 Ritual Tones using the San Fen Sun Yi method of calculation—alternating subtraction and addition of 1/3 the pipe length.

Set the Gong tone (Yellow Bell) pipe length equal to 1; then subtract 1/3 of the Gong pipe and the result is the pipe length of the Zheng tone (the note a fifth higher). Next add 1/3 of the Zheng pipe length to the Zheng pipe and the result is the pipe length of the Shang tone. By repeating this process, all 12 tones are generated. The mathematical formulas are:

1	$1 - (1/3) = 2/3$ $= 0.6666$	$2/3 + (2/3/3) = 8/9$ $= 0.8888$	$8/9 - (8/9/3) = 16/27$ $= 0.5925$	$16/27 + (16/27/3) = 64/81$ $= 0.7901$	...
宮 Gong	徵 Zheng	商 Shang	羽 Yu	角 Jue	

25

Comparing the Relationship of the 12 Ritual Tones and their length ratios using the San Fen Sun Yi process versus the Piano chromatic scale based on Equal Temperament.

Middle C — Note the difference in the ratios between the two — A 440 Hz

	1 C	2 C#	3 D	4 D#	5 E	6 F	7 F#	8 G	9 G#	10 A	11 Bb	12 B	13 C'
12 Ritual Tones	Huang Zhong 黄鐘	Da Lv 大呂	Tai Zhu 大簇	Jia Zhong 夾鐘	Gu Xie 姑洗	Zhong Lv 仲呂	Rui Bin 蕤賓	Lin Zhong 林鐘	Yi Ze 夷則	Nan Lv 南呂	Wu Yi 無射	Ying Zhong 應鐘	Huang Zhong' 黄鐘
	Yang	Yin	Yang	Yin	Yang	Yin	Yang	Yin	Yang	Yin	Yang	Yin	Yang
5-tone scale	Gong		Shang		Jue			Zheng		Yu			Gong'
7-tone scale	Gong 宮		Shang 商		Jue 角		Bian Zheng 變徵	Zheng 徵		Yu 羽		Bian Gong 變宮	Gong' 宮
Tones Using San Fen Sun Yi Tuning Process													
Length ratio	2	1.8728	1.7777	1.6646	1.5802	1.4798	1.4046	1.3333	1.2484	1.1850	1.1098	1.0534	0.9864
CORRESPONDING TONES IN EQUAL TEMPERAMENT TUNING													
Piano notes	C	C#	D	D#	E	F	F#	G	G#	A	Bb	B	C'
Solfège Syllables for the Chromatic and 7-Tone Major Scales													
12 semitones	Do	Di	Re	Ri	Mi	Fa	Fi	Sol	Si	La	Te (or Ta)	Ti	Do'
7-tone scale in key of C	Do		Re		Mi	Fa		Sol		La		Ti	Do'
In key of D		Ti	Do		Re		Mi	Fa		Sol		La	
Tones Using Equal Temperament Tuning													
Length ratio	2	1.8877	1.7817	1.6817	1.5874	1.4983	1.4142	1.3348	1.2599	1.1892	1.1224	1.0594 = $\sqrt[12]{2}$	1
Ratio calculation		2 / 1.05946	1.8877 / 1.05946	1.7817 / 1.05946	1.6817 / 1.05946	1.5874 / 1.05946	1.4983 / 1.05946	1.4142 / 1.05946	1.3348 / 1.05946	1.2599 / 1.05946	1.1892 / 1.05946	1.1224 / 1.05946	1.05946 / 1.05946
Note Frequency*	262 Hz	277 Hz	293 Hz	311 Hz	329 Hz	349 Hz	370 Hz	392 Hz	415 Hz	440 Hz	466 Hz	493 Hz	523 Hz
Calculation	261.63	261.63 x 1.05946= 277.18	277.18x 1.05946= 293.67	293.67 x 1.05946= 311.13	311.13 x 1.05946= 329.63	329.63 x 1.05946= 349.23	349.23 x 1.05946= 369.99	370.00 x 1.05946= 392.00	392.00 x 1.05946= 415.30	415.30 x 1.05946= 440.00	440.00 x 1.05946= 466.16	466.16 x 1.05946= 493.88	493.88 x 1.05946= 523.25

* The frequencies of the 12 semitones in an octave

Addressing the difference between Arithmetic Progression and Geometric Progression

I N Equal Temperament tuning, an octave is divided into a series of 12 equal steps based on mathematical calculations; the 12 steps are equal on a logarithmic scale. For more than two thousand years, Chinese musicians (as well as other cultures) had long been unsuccessful in the search for Musical Equal Temperament that could perpetually generate 12 ritual tones representing the 12 months of the year. They failed to find the proper length or the common frequency ratio between two adjacent tones of the ritual music. Inspired from his father Zhu Houwan and grandfather-in-law He Tang, (both were outstanding musicologists) Zhu Zaiyu took it upon himself to complete this great task. He understood that certain acoustic tones conformed to certain mathematical numbers. Only an authentic mathematical number corresponded well with the authentic tone. He knew that the 3:2 ratio and the *San Fen Sun Yi* process would not produce the desired identical ratio between two adjacent tones because they were derived from the arithmetic progression which produced varying arithmetic means between the adjacent tones. He determined that a different kind of geometric progression ratio was needed to create the equal-distant interval scale system.

Let us put down the series of figures: *2 4 6 8 10 12 14 16 18 20*. This series is called "an arithmetical progression". One can tell that there is a difference of 2, the *common difference*, between two adjacent numbers. But if we put down the series of figures: *2 4 8 16 32 64 128,* we have a totally different situation. The second series is called "a geometrical progression"; we multiply by 2, the *common ratio*, each time. If there are 440 Hz or cps (cycles per second) between the pitches A440 and A880 (the note one octave above

A440) and there are twelve semitones between them, the scale is "a geometrical progression" and the cps for each note above the one adjacent are found by multiplying by some factor or common ratio.

So the best formula to form an equal-distant tonal system in an octave is to find the common ratio of a geometric series of 12 terms. In the book, *The True Essence of Ritual Tone* (*Lv Lv Jing Yi*), published in 1581, musicologist Zhu Zaiyu detailed the mathematical rules of the geometric progression that would break the barriers of the outdated *San Fen Sun Yi* process.

There is a beautiful view beyond the mountain through the eyes of a Genius

Zhu Zaiyu envisioned the necessity of tempering the ritual tones to satisfy the mathematical properties. Discerning the desired equidistant interval scale system required a different kind of progression ratio or proportional relationship between the mathematical calculations and the tone generation. He believed there must be a common ratio among the 12 equidistant semitones in the scale, corresponding to the 12 cyclic months of a year evenly divided, so that the tuning system would allow musicians to freely transpose the melody in any key and to play the major scale in any key.

He set the length for the string or flute of the standard tone to be 1. The length of the next tone one octave lower should be 2. The mathematical ratio of the two notes of the octave is 1:2. If for each semitone its length or frequency is multiplied by an equal number, the intervals between all 12 tones would all be identical, and an equal tempered scale would result. This also would show the concordance between the 12 ritual tone system and 12-month calendar.

Zhu Zaiyu realized the dialectical relationship between a mathematic and acoustic tone. If the tone was not concordant, the mathematical value could be wrong. The practical theory would apply to the mathematical tones for its logical variations. It could not be manually approximated by the *San Fen Sun Yi* method or any other approximate manipulation. In other words, the only absolute way is attained by mathematical calculation.

Zhu Zaiyu initiated the formula for finding the common ratio of a 5-term geometrical series. (With the first and last terms known, one only has to find the remaining 2nd, 3rd and 4th terms of the series.) First, he started by finding the common ratio of the two notes of the octave, which is 1 to 2, and determining the geometric mean or midpoint between them, which is $\sqrt{2}$. This number is the 3rd term of the geometric series. Next, he determined the common ratio (the geometric mean or midpoint) between the midpoint $\sqrt{2}$ and 1 to be $\sqrt{\sqrt{2}}$. Using this same approach, he realized the midpoint between the midpoint $\sqrt{2}$ and 2 to be a square root of $\sqrt{\sqrt{2}}$. The 5-term geometric series thus became 1, $\sqrt{\sqrt{2}}$, $\sqrt{2}$, $\sqrt{2} * \sqrt{\sqrt{2}}$, 2, where the common ratio between each of the five terms is $\sqrt{\sqrt{2}}$. From there, he found the common ratio for the 12-term series by taking a cubic root of the $\sqrt{\sqrt{2}}$ which is $\sqrt[3]{\sqrt{\sqrt{2}}}$ or $\sqrt[12]{2}$. The next chapter outlines the procedure of Zhu Zaiyu's mathematical operation. By using the double-deck abacus, he calculated the 12th root of 2 to an accuracy of 24 decimal places (a 25-digit number). (See page 51 for a picture of a double-deck abacus.)

The picture at the left is named Mi Lv Liu Yuan. *It shows the method of determining the hypotenuse of a right-angled isosceles triangle that divides a circle into two (or four) equal parts. It inspired Zhu Zaiyu to apply its principles in his search for Equal Temperament. Using a Square in a Circle to find the diameter of a circle was developed in the Zhou Dynasty (6th century B.C.)*

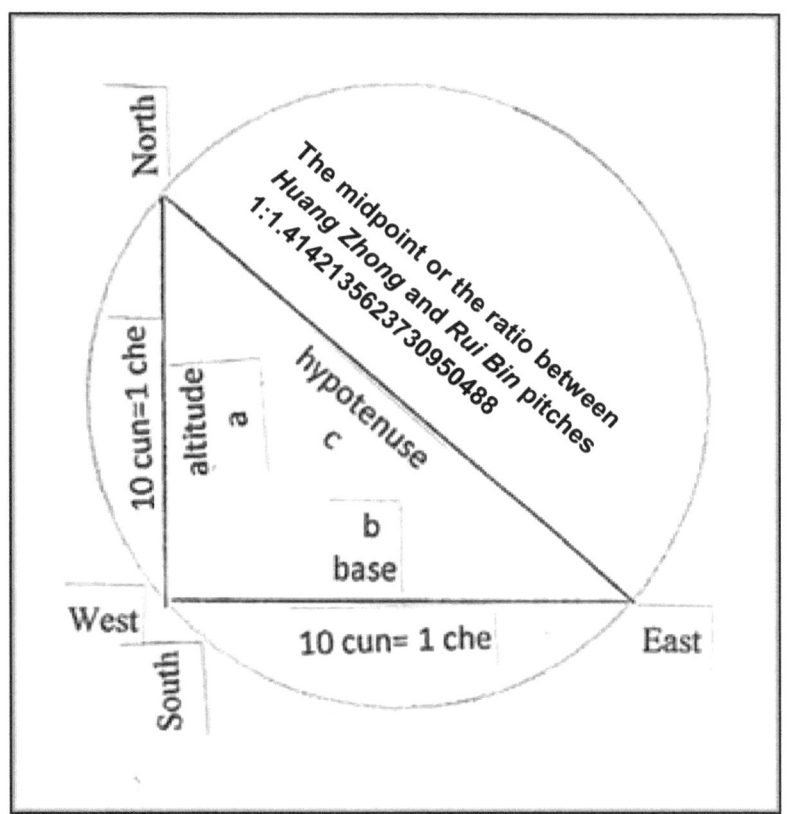

The picture above shows how Zhu Zaiyu determined the midpoint in an octave to be the square root of two by using the Geometric principle that in a right-angled isosceles triangle, $a^2 + b^2 = c^2$. He set $a=b=1$ and got $\sqrt{1 + 1} = \sqrt{2}$

The Mathematical Calculation of the Common Ratio

Key	C4	C4#	D4	D4#	E4	F4	F4#	G4	G4#	A4	A4#	B4	C5
	Huang Zhong	Da Lv	Tai Zhu	Jia Zhong	Gu Xie	Zhong Lv	Rui Bin	Lin Zhong	Yi Ze	Nan Lv	Wu Yi	Ying Zhong	Qing Huang Zhong
Length	2	1.8877	1.7817	1.6817	1.5874	1.4983	1.4142	1.3348	1.2599	1.1892	1.1224	1.0594	1

1. **Determining the midpoint of an octave to be the square root of 2, by using the hypotenuse of a right-angled isosceles triangle.** Starting with the equation, $a^2 + b^2 = c^2$, and setting a = b = 1, the solution for c is found: $1 + 1 = c^2$, $c = \sqrt{1 + 1} = \sqrt{2} =$ 1.414213562373. This number represents the note (*Rui Bin* or F4♯) exactly at the midpoint between the fundamental note *Huang Zhong* (which is 2, or the note C4 on the piano keyboard) and the note Qing *Huang Zhong* (which is 1 and an octave above *Huang Zhong*, or the note C5 on the piano keyboard). The distance between this midpoint to each of the two end-notes of the octave is exactly equal and can be shown mathematically. By multiplying the starting note (*Qing Huang Zhong* or C5) by the common distance between it and the midpoint, the result is the frequency of the midpoint (*Rui Bin* or F4♯): $1 * \sqrt{2} = \sqrt{2}$. Repeating this method, the midpoint (Rui Bin or F4♯) multiplied by the common distance ratio gives the result of the frequency of the other end-note of the octave (Huang Zhong or C4): $\sqrt{2} * \sqrt{2} = 2$. It also indicates a year divided into two equinoxes.) $\sqrt{2}$ **is the midpoint between 2 and 1.**

2. **Using the same procedure to determine the midpoint between *Qing Huang Zhong* (C5) and *Rui Bin* (F4♯).** Since the calculation of the midpoint between the two end-notes (1 and 2) of the octave yielded $\sqrt{2}$, it follows that the midpoint between the end-notes 1 (Qing *Huang Zhong* or C5) and the newly calculated midpoint $\sqrt{2}$ (Rui Bin or F4♯) is the square root of the $\sqrt{2}$ which is

$\sqrt{\sqrt{2}} = \sqrt{1.41421\ldots} = 1.189207\ldots$ This number represents the note (Nan Lv or A4) which is exactly at the midpoint between the notes C5 and F4♯. Again the distance between this midpoint to each of the two end-notes (Qing Huang Zhong or C5 and Rui Bin or F4♯) is an equal ratio which forms the interval of a minor third (containing 3 semitones) between the notes C5 and A4 or between the notes A4 and F4♯. (It also indicates the position of the two solstices equally between the two equinoxes.) $\sqrt{\sqrt{2}}$ **is the midpoint between** $\sqrt{2}$ **and 1**.

3. **Finding the ratio for a semitone**. Having divided an octave into four equal parts by the two calculations described above, each of the four parts would now need to be divided into three equal parts for there to be 12 notes in the space of an octave. This time the calculation would need to locate a point that is one-third (instead of one-half) the distance between the notes Qing Huang Zhong or C5 and Nan Lv or A4. To determine the point one-third of the distance of the interval of a minor third, the calculation needed to be the cube root of $\sqrt{\sqrt{2}}$ which is $\sqrt[3]{\sqrt{\sqrt{2}}} = \sqrt[3]{1.189207\ldots} =$ 1.059463094.... This same calculation $(\sqrt[3]{\sqrt{\sqrt{2}}})$ can also be written as the 12th root of 2 or $\sqrt[12]{2} = 1.059463094\ldots$ By multiplying 1.059463094 times itself 11 times we get 2. This number is the correct ratio for generating the equal-tempered tonal series. Thus each note in the scale is an equidistant from the adjacent notes. **1.059463094... is the ratio for the semitone**.

Illustration applying the Magic Number: 1.059463094 times itself 11 times = 2 (or 1.059463094^{12}=2)

1. The first calculation found the midpoint between 1 and 2, which is $\sqrt{2}$. This is the midpoint note F4# between the notes of the octave C4 and C5 on the piano keyboard (the midpoint note Rui Bin between the Chinese fundamental note *Huang Zhong* and Qing (double) *Huang Zhong*).

   $\sqrt{2}$=1.4142135 = the length of the note F4# (*Rui Bin*) ❶

2. The second calculation found the midpoint between $\sqrt{2}$ and 1, which is $\sqrt{\sqrt{2}}$ or $\sqrt[4]{2}$. This is the midpoint note A4 between the notes F4# and C5 on the piano keyboard (the midpoint note *Nan Lv* between *Rui Bin* and *Qing Huang Zhong*).

   $\sqrt[4]{2}$ =1.189207 = the length of the note A4 (Nan Lv) ❷

3. The third calculation took a cubic root of $\sqrt[4]{2}$ which is $\sqrt[3]{\sqrt[4]{2}}$. This produced the common ratio between $\sqrt{\sqrt{2}}$ (the note A4) and 1(the note C5), which divides that length (known as the interval of a minor third) into three equal segments (known as semitones).

   $$\sqrt[3]{\sqrt[4]{2}} = \sqrt[12]{2} = \sqrt[3]{\sqrt{\sqrt{2}}}= \sqrt[3]{1.189207 \ldots}= 1.059463094\ldots$$

This number for the 12th root of 2 is the common ratio between successive notes that divide one octave into 12 equal parts or, in other words, it is the building block for producing an equal-distant 12-tone scale. This is how it works.

- **For a Geometrical progression series**: Each number in the series is a multiple of a constant common factor or ratio. For example, in the series 1 2 4 8 16 32 64 128 256 512 1024 2048 4096 ... the common ratio is 2. By multiplying any number in the series by the common ratio, the result is the next number in the series. Another way to describe this series is that it is the result of repeatedly multiplying a common ratio times itself. The mathematical designation for the progression in this example is 2^n.

- **For an Equal Temperament series of 12 semitones within an octave**: The calculation using a geometric progression would start with the first term 1 and end with the last term 2. When the fundamental value 1 is multiplied by the common ratio 1.059463094 twelve times, the product is 2. However, before starting this process, there are some issues in terminology that need to be addressed to reduce confusion.

It is important to note that the first calculation in a geometric progression establishes the second term of the series and it is the common ratio for the series. (The series begins from a starting point of 1 which acts as zero, because in mathematical notation any number to the power of zero (n^0) is equal to 1.) It is not until the calculation is done a second time (to determine the third term in the series) that the common ratio is multiplied times itself. For each term in the series thereafter, the pervious term is multiplied by the common ratio which is the same as multiplying the common ration times itself one more time. That is the reason why thirteen terms (or notes) are used to identify the 12 "different" notes in the 12-tone scale within the space of an octave, the mathematical notation for the geometric progression is 1.0594630964^{12} and the common ration of 1.0594630964 times itself 11 times all culminate at 2, which is the note an octave from the starting note. The calculation of the progression looks like this:

1 * 1.059463 = 1.059463 (or 1.059463^1). [The second term of the progression]
[The next step is the first time the common ratio is multiplied times itself.]
1.059463 * 1.059463 = 1.1224 (or 1.059463^2) [The third term of the progression]
1.1224 * 1.059463 = 1.1892 (or 1.059463^3 = 1.059463*1.059463*1.059463)

1.1892 * 1.059463 = 1.2599 (or 1.059463^4 =
1.059463*1.059463*1.059463*1.059463)

... and so on for eight more times, producing the series:
1 1.05946 1.1224 1.1892 1.2599 1.3348 1.4142 1.4983
1.5874 1.6817 1.7817 1.8877 2.

The mathematical designation for this progression is
1.059463094^{12}. The diagram below shows how both the length
and the frequency of each pitch in the 12-tone scale are
multiples of the common ratio.

Using an abacus, Zhu Zaiyu calculated the common ratio or identical
frequency ratio to be 1.0594630943592952645618825. This magic
number was named *Mi Lv* 密率 by Zhu Zaiyu.

Semitones	12	11	10	9	8	7	6	5	4	3	2	1	0
Note	C4	C4#	D4	D4#	E4	F4	F4#	G4	G4#	A4	A4#	B4	C5
Chinese Name	Huang Zhong	Da Lv	Tai Zhu	Jia Zhong	Gu Xie	Zhong Lv	Rui Bin	Lin Zhong	Yi Ze	Nan Lv	Wu Yi	Ying Zhong	Qing Huang Zhong
Solfège Name	Do	Di	Re	Ri	Mi	Fa	Fi	Sol	Si	La	Te (Ta)	Ti	Do'
Length	2	1.8877 $2\sqrt[3]{(\sqrt[4]{2})}$	1.7817	1.6817 $\sqrt[4]{2}x\sqrt{2}$	1.5874	1.4983	1.4142 $\sqrt{2}$	1.3348	1.2599	1.1892 $\sqrt{(\sqrt{2})}$	1.1224	1.059463 $\sqrt[3]{(\sqrt[4]{2})}$	1
Length as multiple of common ratio	$(\sqrt[12]{2})^{12}$ = 2	$(\sqrt[12]{2})^{11}$	$(\sqrt[12]{2})^{10}$	$(\sqrt[12]{2})^{9}$	$(\sqrt[12]{2})^{8}$	$(\sqrt[12]{2})^{7}$	$(\sqrt[12]{2})^{6}$	$(\sqrt[12]{2})^{5}$	$(\sqrt[12]{2})^{4}$	$(\sqrt[12]{2})^{3}$	$(\sqrt[12]{2})^{2}$	$(\sqrt[12]{2})^{1}$	$(\sqrt[12]{2})^{0}$ = 1
Note Frequency	262 Hz	277 Hz	293 Hz	311 Hz	329 Hz	349 Hz	370 Hz	392 Hz	415 Hz	440 Hz	466 Hz	493 Hz	523 Hz
Multiply by Frequency ratio 1.05946	261.63	261.63 x 1.05946 277.18	277.18 x 1.05946 293.67	293.67 x 1.05946 311.13	311.13 x 1.05946 329.63	329.63 x 1.05946 349.23	349.23 x 1.05946 369.99	370.00 x 1.05946 392.00	392.00 x 1.05946 415.30	415.30 x 1.05946 440.00	440.00 x 1.05946 466.16	466.16 x 1.05946 493.88	493.88 x 1.05946 523.25

Denotes the common ration of $\sqrt[12]{2}$ (which is 1.059463094...) between each of the 12 semitones

What was the motive that prompted Zhu Zaiyu to discover Equal Temperament?

There were two factors that enlightened him to take the challenge:

1. The sprouts of capitalism and the prosperity of city life promoted the development of qualitative art for literature, opera, music, dance, ballad singing and musical instruments in the Ming Dynasty. Cities attracted millions of immigrant workers from different rural areas. They brought along their musical instruments and local operas with different tunings and began to join in the cities' local ballad singings and operas. The demand for a standard tonal system, as well as simpler methods of tonal transposition for musical instruments, was truly needed in order for them to intertwine or form a cohesive performance. It appeared that the requisite for finding a better musical temperament was even more imminent when the commodity economy started developing forward. The renascent development of art science enabled Zhu Zaiyu to be the first person to climb up the stairway trying to reach the pinnacle of Equal Temperament.

2. From scientific and cultural stand points, history tended to focus on the circumstantial conditions of an outstanding inventor or creator. In discovering Equal Temperament, Zhu Zaiyu was richly endowed by the excellent environment surrounding him. He received insightful guidance from his father, Zhu Houwan, a vassal king who was proficient in the Ritual Tonal Temperament System. He also was inspired by the writings from his grandfather-in-law, He Tang, who was an expert on researching and developing the Ritual Equal-Tonal Temperament System. Zhu Zaiyu had a profound respect for his father and grandfather-in-

law. Professor Dai Nianzu, a Zhu Zaiyu biographer, affirmed that the major factor which motivated Zhu Zaiyu to create Equal Temperament laid not only on his industrious study, but also on his unique thinking and commentating approaches to acquiring his forefathers' experiences and lessons. He envisioned the breakthrough by objectively repudiating the erroneous methods adopted by his forefathers. He also justified his vision by reviewing the entire works of ritual tonal temperament from different dynasties.

Designing and building Tuning Instruments to verify the Equal Temperament Theory

ZHU ZAIYU dedicated his life to studying musical temperament theory and putting the theory into practice. He proved the correctness of this new tonal system by building practical musical instruments and composing music for entertaining performances. He created the tuning stringed instrument, *Jun Zhun* 均准, and the tuning pitch pipe, *Lv Guan* 律管, to verify the validity of Equal Temperament (or the Equidistant Tonal System).

The *Jun Zhun* is the name for Zhu Zaiyu's tuning stringed instrument. It had 12 strings with engraved emblems on the sound board under the strings. The strings were the same thickness as those on the zither. The string length was determined from the fundamental tone *Huang Zhong* generated by means of the pitch pipe. Zhu Zaiyu realized that Equal Temperament was not popularly accepted, but the sole purpose of making the *Jun Zhun* was to prove the validity of Equal Temperament. For better understanding of the two musical temperaments, specific markings of the mathematical ratios for all the ritual tones obtained from both the *San Fen Sun Yi* and Equal Temperament tuning methods were carved on the sound board of the instrument. The *Jun Zhun* was not only a stringed instrument; it was also the very first musical instrument tuned with Equal Temperament in the World.

The *Lv Guan*. In his book, *Lv Lv Jing Yi*, Zhu Zaiyu described the procedures of making a *Lv Guan.* It even included the method for selecting the right kind of bamboo pipes based on the homogeneous quality and dimension, filing and adjusting the embouchures, maintaining a correct gesture for blowing the tuning flute and testing and verifying the correct pitches. The tuning pitch pipes he designed spanned 3 octaves. The ascending chromatic tones were proportional to the length of the open-ended pitch pipes based on the mathematical calculation of Equal Temperament; the higher the tones, the shorter the length of the pipe. By carefully filing and adjusting the inner and outer diameters of each pipe, the set of 36 pitch pipes with conical embouchures could precisely sound the desired ritual tones. He suggested that the pitch pipe be held properly straight without covering the lower open end. He also reminded the player to touch the embouchure of the vertical flute with the lower lip and to blow gently without covering more than half the open embouchure in order that the accurate tone could be heard.

Lv Guan
(36 tuning pitch pipes)

Jun Zhun
Back side   Front side

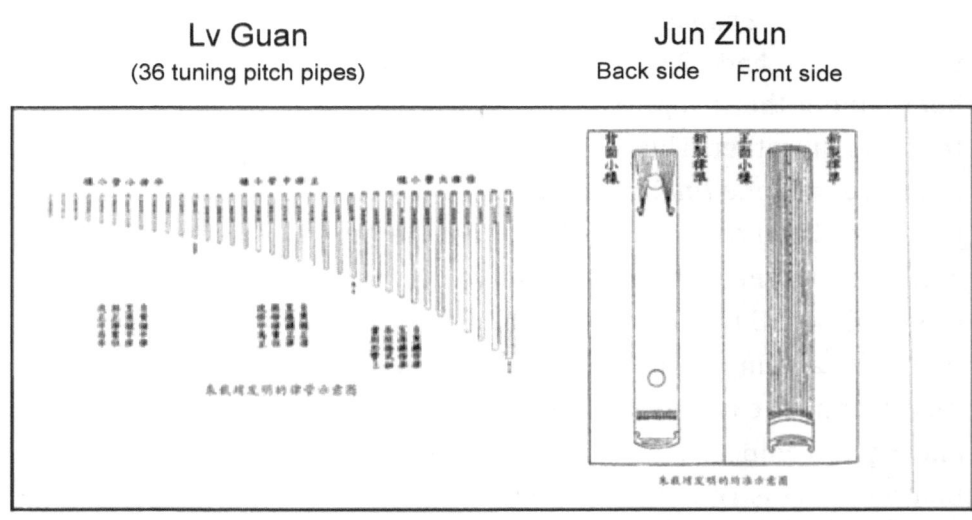

The drawing on the top right is the tuning stringed instrument called Jun Zhun *with 12 strings that can play 12 chromatic tones (C, Db, D, Eb, E, F, F♯, G, Ab, A, Bb, B) in an octave. The 12 insignias on the front side can function like the 12 tones in an octave or the 7 white keys and 5 black keys that form one octave on the modern piano. The drawing on the top left is the tuning pitch pipes called* Lv Guan *consisting of 36 pitch pipes with conical embouchure which can precisely sound the desired 12 chromatic ritual tones over a span of 3 octaves.*

Tuning Instruments

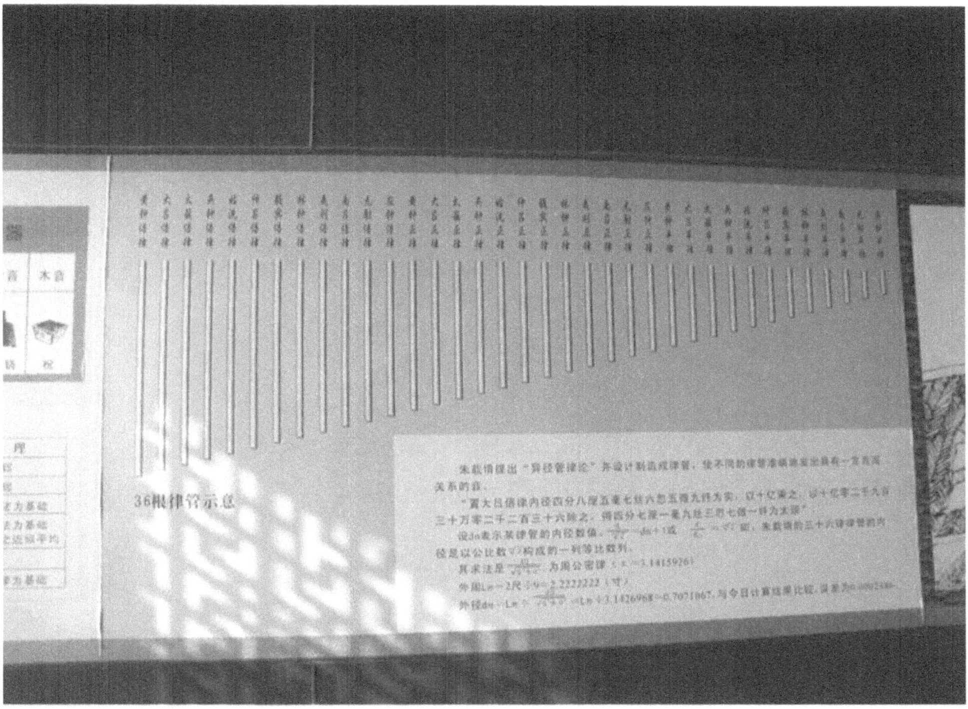

Lv Guan 律管, *The Tuning Pitch Pipes.*

Jun Zhun 均准, *The Tuning Stringed Instrument* .

Modern Piano Tuning in Equal Temperament

Construction of the Circle of Fifths diagrams to show the ease of transposing music and modulating melodies

THE 12-tone scale based on the *San Fen Sun Yi* process was not an equal-distant tonal system because the frequency ratio was not a constant. It failed to restore the fundamental Yellow Bell (*Huang Zhong*) pitch after 12 successive spirals of a perfect fifth starting from Yellow Bell. Equal Temperament provided the advantage of dividing the octave into equal intervals with a constant ratio between each note and made it possible for the 12 ritual tone scale to return to the fundamental Yellow Bell (*Huang Zhong)* pitch one octave higher. Zhu Zaiyu faithfully created the tonal equal-temperament theory based on mathematical calculation. He also diligently implemented his theory with practical experiments.

He created the Circle of Fifths in 1580 to show the relationships among the 12 ritual tones and the corresponding notes

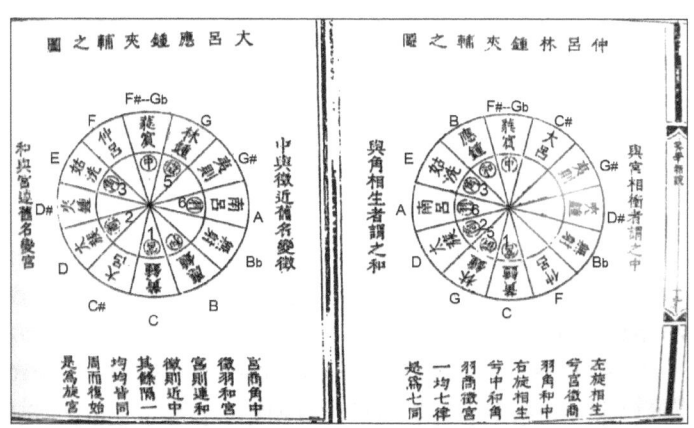

that produce the 7-note scale starting on each ritual tone. This circle portrayed that ascending by a sequence of twelve fifths from any pitch, one returned to exactly the same note as the initial starting tone only at a pitch exactly seven octaves above it. In his book, *New Discourse on Mathematics* （*Suan Xue Xin Shuo*), Zhu Zaiyu drew the Circle of Fifths diagrams to demonstrate the total harmonic freedom, melody modulation and the key note changes provided by the Equidistant Tonal System.

There were inner and outer circles in the Circle of Fifths. The stationary outer circle represented the 12 ritual tones with Yellow Bell (Huang Zhong) positioned in the center at the bottom. The movable inner circle contained the Chinese 7-tone scale. In the left diagram the 12 ritual tones are presented as a 12-tone chromatic scale—each tone is a semitone from the adjacent tone. In the right diagram the 12 ritual tones are presented as the circle of fifths (C-G-D-A-E-B-F♯-C♯-G♯-D♯-B♭-F-C). The movable inner circle, containing the Chinese 7-tone scale, showed in the left diagram the notes progressing clockwise from the fundamental tone "C" in the order the notes appear in the scale, but in the right diagram they are "out of order" as they progress in a series of fifths (1-5-2-6-3-7-4). In both diagrams the inner circle could be rotated so that the fundamental tone "C" (the key note of the 7-tone scale) could be placed to correspond to each of the 12 different tones in the outer circle, the effect of which modulated the melody. The term "fifth" defines the interval or mathematical ratio which is the closest and most consonant non-octave interval. Thus, the Circle of Fifths is a circle of closely-related pitches or key tonalities appearing adjacent to one another. Musicians and composers use the Circle of Fifths to understand and describe those relationships. The circle's design is helpful in composing and harmonizing melodies, building chords and moving (modulating) to different keys within a composition. (Note: Scholar Zhu Xi in the Song Dynasty also proposed the use of the Circle of Fifths to find the fundamental tone of the music melody.)

Today the Circle of Fifths is still used for the same purposes, but it has been adjusted by including the key signatures that correspond to each of the 12 tones and associated major and minor keys to reflect what is referred to as tonality. The outer circle, with the fundamental tone "C" positioned in the center at the top, also displays the key signature which is associated with each tone when a scale begins with that note as its fundamental or key tone. The key signature indicates which notes in the 7-tone scale need to be altered in order to maintain the same pattern of sound, called a major scale in Western music, when the scale starts with each note in the circle as the fundamental key tone. With the key signatures showing what the 7 notes in the major scale are as the fundamental note changes, the inner circle is used to show the note that is the fundamental key tone of a scale which uses the same key signature as the major scale (and therefore includes the same notes) but produces the pattern of sound called a minor scale in Western music. Since the desired related note is always the same as the sixth note in the major scale, the inner circle does not move; it remains stationary so that it can indicate the related or relative minor key associated with each major key and vice versa. Between the two circles there is sometimes a quick reference showing the number of notes that are adjusted in order to produce the same scale pattern when starting from the other notes in the circle as when the scale started on C, and also indicating which direction the adjustment is made from their natural (♮) position in the "C" scale—raised a semitone (sharped or ♯) or lowered a semitone (flatted or ♭).

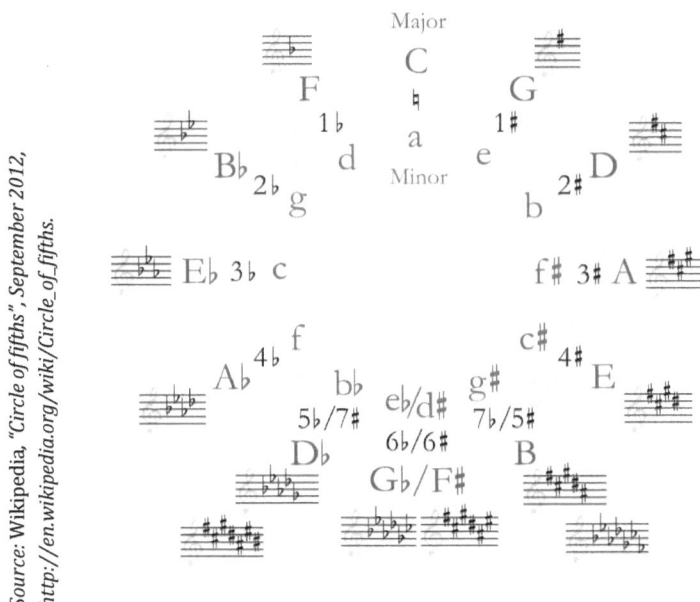

Who contributed to the world of music?

T HE search for Equal Temperament and standard tone is not a simple issue of pure science. Any person who addresses this issue must possess profound knowledge of music and study and investigate the history of various instruments. Zhu Zaiyu had attained a solid foundation in science, applied mathematics and musicology when he was a teenager. His research skills were at a level that hardly anyone could reach.

Looking at the proverbial sky of human history, how many superstars have been born to accomplish such versatile achievements? When Zhu Zaiyu was looking up at the twinkling stars, the vast sky had so many astronomical puzzles for him to ponder, both in the day and in the night. Similarly, there were many scientific and artistic treasures for him to explore on earth. He sought out the truths of nature that rested beyond the boundless sky. For two thousand years, China had relentlessly pursued a tuning system that would permit transposition of the perpetual fundamental tone for the ritual music. Zhu Zaiyu successfully achieved the goal by creating Equal Temperament, which revolutionized the music in Europe as well as China. However, Equal Temperament Tuning was rejected blindly by the ignorant court officers, in both the Ming and Qing dynasties, who treasured and worshipped the less accurate *San Fen Sun Yi* process. Equal Temperament is a great achievement in music, but Zhu Zaiyu's findings were almost forgotten due to this lack of recognition by his rulers, and there was no successor after him. Only a few scholars acknowledged and appreciated the academic value of the musical theory during his lifetime.

The piano was invented by Italian Bartolomeo Cristofori in the 18th century. It became one of the world's most-familiar musical instruments because of its versatility and ubiquity. The piano was tuned with the standard Equal Temperament scale which produced rich overtones and harmonics that the piano uniquely possesses. Each note shines more brilliantly in the other's company when the piano is tuned with Equal Temperament; it would not sound as well if the piano were tuned to the pitches in the Mean Tone scale because it lacks pleasing harmonics. This was the principal reason that Bach discerned the exceptional quality of sound that a piano in tempered tuning had and how easily it could play in all 24 keys; in order to demonstrate the piano's versatility, he went ahead and composed *The Well-Tempered Clavier* which became one of the world's great intellectual treasures.

It seems hard for many people, including the Chinese, to believe the Equal Temperament tuning system was invented by a Ming Prince. However, Zhu Zaiyu's contribution to the modern world has been recognized by Dr. Joseph Needham, a British scientist, historian and Sinologist known for his scientific research and writing on the history of Chinese science. Dr. Needham asserted that Zhu Zaiyu was the very first person to invent the Equal Temperament theory based on mathematical calculation. In addition, the 19th-century, noted German physicist, Hermann von Helmholtz, in his book, *On the Sensations of Tone as a Physiological Basis for the Theory of Music*, wrote that "a certain Chinese Prince Tsai-Yu [Zaiyu] introduced a scale of seven notes, and the division of the Octave into twelve Semitones was discovered by this intelligent and skillful nation".

Visitors can witness Zhu Zaiyu's lifetime academic works of arts and science at the Zhu Zaiyu Memorial in Qinyang city, in Henan Province of Central China. The epic documents and artifacts it displays includes his masterpiece, *The Complete Edition of the Ritual Tone System* (*Yue Lv Quan Shu*), and the tuning instruments he built to verify the Equal Temperament theory, as well as the double-deck 81-digit abacus he used to calculate the 12th root of 2. The exhibition also shows his versatile accomplishments in mathematics, astronomy, physics, dancing, poetry and musical instruments. Zhu

Zaiyu was a humble person and did not have a material legacy of wealth or estate. He did not even know his creative spirit and accomplishments contributed so much to modern mankind.

As human civilization continues to advance, we are in an ever-changing space age of living where science and technology have elevated to another orbit. People live longer lives but with more stress; communication has advanced from paper to wireless electronic pads; sparks of entertaining firecrackers have evolved into lethal bombs; and so on. The only thing that is impervious to the ravages of time is the principle of Music. It cannot be eroded by chemicals or technology; rather, it generates humanism, feelings and emotions that science cannot duplicate. Zhu Zaiyu, a Chinese prince of the Ming Dynasty, planted the seeds of music as we know it today, and then European musicians and composers cultivated and bore the fruits of his ideas. In this way, East and West worked together to create the sound of music for the entire world.

The Zhu Zaiyu Memorial Museum

Z HU ZAIYU MEMORIAL MUSEUM was constructed over the ancient site where Marquis Zheng's Royal Court was located during the Ming dynasty. The museum serves not only as an institute for scholars to study Zhu Zaiyu's lifetime achievements, but also serves as a cultural center for carrying forward the prolific and magnificent achievements of the Chinese civilization. Both Zhu Zaiyu and his father, Zhu Houwan (also called Zheng Gong), who was a provincial king, studied the calendar system, the ritual tonal system and ritual dance at the Royal court. The museum displays are grouped as follows:

The 1st exhibition room: Presents the historical and cultural backgrounds of Qinyang City, showing and telling the life of Zhu Zaiyu, as well as the family background of the royal Marquis Zheng.

The 2nd exhibition room: Unfolds in detail the life of Zhu Zaiyu and the hardships he encountered. The displays also reveal his endeavors and his quest to understand the ritual tonal system and astronomical knowledge.

The 3rd exhibition room: Illustrates how Zhu Zaiyu developed the theory and calculation of Equal Temperament. Displays show his versatile accomplishments in mathematics, astronomy, physics, dancing, poetry and musical instruments, as well as his contributions to modern music and science.

The 4th exhibition room: Exhibits art by modern painters and calligraphers commemorating the memory of Zhu Zaiyu with much praise and appreciation.

Zhu Zaiyu Museum Pictures

T HE ZHU ZAIYU MEMORIAL MUSEUM is located in Qinyang City, Henan Province, China.

Music Sage, Zhu Zaiyu.

The double-deck 81-digit abacus Zhu Zaiyu used to calculate the 12th root of 2. $^{12}\sqrt{2}$ = 1.059463094359295264561825.

The Complete Edition of the Ritual Tone System, Yue Lv Quan Shu 樂律全書. *The series includes the 36 books first issued in 1581.*

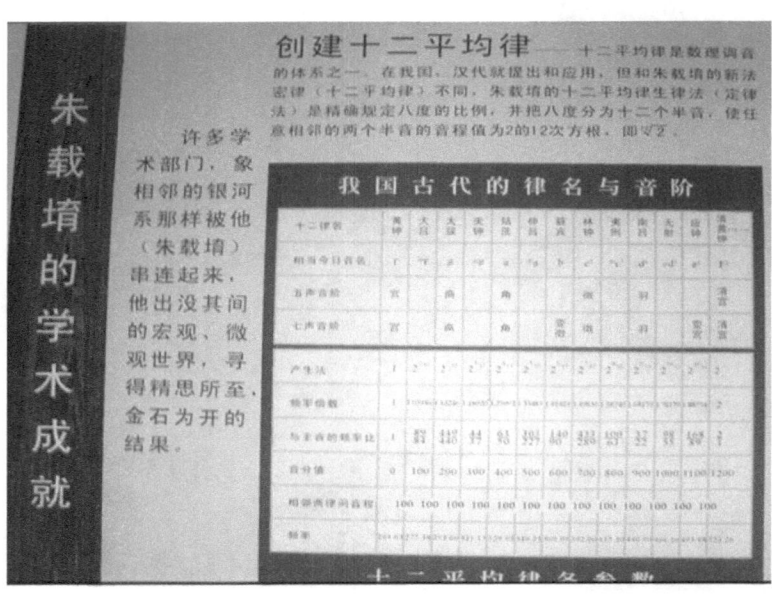

Ancient China's 12 Ritual Tones and the modern Chromatic Scale with 12 semitones.

References

1. *The Complete Edition of the Ritual Tone System* by Zhu Zaiyu (1581)
2. *History of Acoustics in China* by Dai Nianzu (1998)
3. *The Immortal True Man Zhu Zaiyu* by Dai Nianzu (2011)
4. *The Discovery of Musical Temperament in China and Europe* by Gene Cho (2003)
5. *Music sage Zhu Zaiyu* compiled by Du Jingli (2006)
6. *A study of Musical Temperament in East and West* by Guang-Qi Wang (1936)
7. *The Genius of China* by Robert Temple (1986)
8. *Wikipedia, "Well Temperament", http://en.wikipedia.org/.wiki/ Well_temperament,* September, 2012
9. *On the Sensations of Tone as a Psychological Basis for the Theory of Music* by Hermann von Helmholtz (1954)
10. *Tuning and Temperament* by J. Murray Bardour (2004)
11. *Science and Civilization in China,* Vol IV:1 (Physics), Joseph Needham, Cambridge University Press, 1962- 2004, pp 220 ff.
12. Brandy Kraemer, "Scientific Note Number", http://0.tqn.com/d/ piano/1/0/T/F/-/-/Piano-Key-Names-SPN_large.png, 1 October 2012.
13. *Wikipedia,* "Circle of fifths", http://en.wikipedia.org/wiki/ Circle_of_fifths, September, 2012

www.ingramcontent.com/pod-product-compliance
Lightning Source LLC
Chambersburg PA
CBHW021252280526
45784CB00005B/2338